To Boston with Love

The story of the first woman
to run the Boston Marathon

by Bobbi Gibb

50th Anniversary Edition

Foreword (50th Anniversary Edition)

When I first saw the Boston Marathon in 1964, I fell in love with the event and the runners. It was totally irrational because I didn't know anything about road races or marathons as organized competitions, but I instantly felt that the runners in the race must feel exactly the same way I felt when I was running through the woods and around Boston. I recognized them as kindred spirits. I felt that they were running with joy, and also living a life of endurance and integrity.

When I joined in with the runners in Hopkinton in 1966, they proved what I had imagined. They were so excited and welcoming to have me with them.

Fifty years later, I still feel the same way about the Boston Marathon. When I watch the finishers, I sometimes break into tears. They are so tired and exhausted, yet they have succeeded at something wonderful. And their fatigue will soon end, and in another year they will return again for the wonderful celebration of spring and life and renewed friendships that the Boston Marathon represents.

The runners, the spectators, the Boston organizers-- everyone is so supportive of everyone else. That's the way I've always imagined life and community and men-and-women-together should be. That's why I continue to love the Boston Marathon as much as I did 50 years ago.

-Bobbi Gibb, April 2016

Bobbi Gibb
Grand Marshal of the 2016 Boston Marathon

I ran the Boston Marathon out of love. I believe that love is the basis of all meaningful human endeavor.

Running expresses my love of Nature, my delight in being alive. Yet it was a love that was incomplete until it was shared with others.

When I started running, I knew no other runners, male or female. I had not heard of the Boston Marathon and had never seen a track meet.

I ran as a way of reaffirming some semiconscious ancient bond between the Earth and myself as a human animal.

I came to running from a feeling that something was missing in my secure suburban existence and in the life plan the 1950's had in store for me.

At a deeper level I sought to come to terms with my own mortality, with the relationship between mind or soul and body or the physical. I was groping for a synthesis in my life and found comfort in running long-distance through field, forest and city. I was looking for the bare reality of things, people, and the world. That comprehension excited and awed me.

My running companions were my dog and her canine friends.

I found peace in the solitude and exquisite perfection of Nature.

As a student at Tufts University School of Special Studies, I met a man who ran cross-country.

"Five miles!" I exclaimed in disbelief when he told me how long the meet was.

But within six months I was trotting right along as he ran five, six, ten miles.

I seemed to have a knack for it and a lot of stamina.

"Twenty-six miles!" I gasped when the father of a friend told me about the Boston Marathon in 1964.

"Sure. Why don't you go out and watch it since you like running so much," he suggested.

At that time I was commuting eight miles from Winchester to Boston, running, every day.

So I went, and I saw people running. They looked like wonderful people, like some kind of exotic animal running so strongly, quietly, patiently.

I knew they felt the same bond as I felt with some ancient human potential all but lost in modern society.

I recognized a kindredness with these runners and some internal decision was made to run with them in a mutual expression of our belief in what it means to be human.

I started to train but had no coach, no notion of how to train, no encourage-ment, no role models. So I just kept running farther and farther, curious to see how far I could go and how fast.

Some days I could fly like a bird, other days I felt tired and discouraged.

My friend and I explored the architectural wonders of Boston, New York, and New Haven together. We ran out along the railroad tracks, across frozen lakes. He would take me into the country and drop me off to run home.

That summer I took my dog and VW bus across the continent to California and back, running every day in a new place.

The hills of Pennsylvania and West Virginia, the lush forests of Indiana, the plains of Kansas and Nebraska, the streets of Denver, the high meadows of the Rockies, the Sierras and the Coastal Mountains of California all became my friends.

Miles and miles of nameless trails I ran, and at night I slept under the stars.

The next April, 1965, I stood almost in tears watching the Marathon with two sprained ankles. It would be another year before I ran.

That autumn, still training, I ran sixty-five miles of the Woodstock Vermont hundred-mile equestrian event, in which the horses run 40 miles the first day, 40 miles the second day and 20 miles the third day.

The first day I arose at dawn and set off with the first horses. All day we ran over rugged terrain, dirt roads and mountain trails.

The horses and riders passed me and at lunchtime they stopped and I passed them. The riders were friendly. Often we would converse as I trotted along beside their horses. We finished around 1:00 p.m.

The next day I set off again at dawn and ran 25 miles before my knees started hurting. Many years later I was to discover that running on my toes, as I did, strained my knees.

A good coach is invaluable to a runner.

I hitchhiked back to the barn with a trucker who accepted my "eccentric" passion for running with the usual Yankee understatement.

"Better luck next year," he smiled as he dropped me off, as if running 40 miles in one day and 65 miles in two days over rough terrain, old logging roads and incredible hills was some kind of failure.

Finally, in February 1966, I wrote for my application for the Boston Marathon from California, where I had moved.

I received a curt reply that women were not physiologically able to run such distances and furthermore were not allowed to do so.

I was stunned. I'd heard that the Marathon was open to every person in the world. It had never crossed my mind to consider myself different from the other runners.

My outrage turned to humor as I thought how many preconceived prejudices would crumble when I trotted right along for twenty-six miles.

I knew nothing of the formal world of athletics. No doubt people of the time, both men and women, simply didn't know. Women in sports were not allowed to run more than one and a half miles. Women not in sports would have little reason to do so.

My running of the Marathon thus became a feminist statement. I believed that once people knew women could run marathon distances, the field would naturally open up. I even dreamed of running an Olympic marathon.

Boston is my home and the Boston Marathon has a special significance to me. I ran it three times.

I'll never forget my first run in 1966; popcorn vendors, balloons, kids, crowds of people!

Still tired from riding the bus four days and three nights from California to Boston, I had disguised myself in a blue hooded sweatshirt and was wearing new boys' size six running shoes. (Women's running shoes weren't made then.)

The look on my mother's face as she dropped me off in Hopkinton reflected pride and concern, a combination of "I know you can do it" and "Will you be all right?"

The other runners were clustered in the starting pen. I was crouched in the bushes.

"Bang!" the starting gun fired.

I stumbled from the bushes into the midst of the runners, wondering how many other women writers, artists, scientists, and soldiers had had to disguise their femininity; so well that history has still not discovered.

I have since come to see how history can be distorted merely by repetition of a non-truth by a person or group with a financial or egotistical reason for doing so, or simply through carelessness.

My heart was beating double time as I began to realize the implications of what I was attempting.

I tend to be shy, and here I was in front of thousands of people. A pang of loneliness shot through my gut.

After a few miles, I noticed a studious silence behind me, and murmurs.

"Is that a girl?"

"Hmmm."

"It is a girl!"

I turned and smiled over my shoulder.

They laughed and so did I.

"Hey, fantastic!" they said.

"Are you going to run the whole way?" they asked.

"I hope so," I replied.

"That's great! I wish more women ran."

"I wish my wife would run," one man said wistfully.

I felt these men were my brothers. I could see how much they wanted to share their passion for running with the women in their lives.

As I warmed up, I began to want to take off my sweatshirt and its constricting hood.

"Go ahead," the tall man from Connecticut said.

"I'm afraid if they know I'm a woman they will throw me out," I confessed.

"We won't let them," one said.

"It's a free road," said another.

As soon as the crowds saw I was a woman there was a great commotion. People yelled and cheered, calling out to me, wishing me good luck.

I wanted to respond, to say "Thank you," and to smile and wave back.

"How rude to run right by," I thought.

Mr. Chamberlain, the tall man from Connecticut, ran stride for stride with me for some nineteen miles.

We chatted on and off. His presence gave me comfort. My dream was that men and women could run together and share the consciousness of the common bond of humanity based on a mutual commitment and sharing of what they love in life.

Hatred, war between the sexes, exhausts both and leads to nothing.

We were churning off each mile in a little less than seven minutes.

As we passed Wellesley College, women waved and shouted in exultation.

I felt as though I was setting these women free. I was touched that my running meant so much to them.

One woman, with several children clinging to her ample coat, called ecstatically, "Ave Maria, Ave Maria!"

I felt a surge of tears come to my eyes at the contact. Did she know that in my heart I wanted children; that I respected her for her devotion, patience, and her strength? She had undertaken, without thought of fame or reward, the most difficult, most important human endeavor of all.

Twenty miles and I felt splendid. I was conserving my energy now, aware that if I failed to finish I would end up disproving exactly what I had set out to prove and would support rather than demolish the then-current prejudices and precon- ceptions about women.

So I didn't push but ran comfortably until the bottoms of my feet began to burn.

I wasn't used to running on pavement and my new shoes hurt. Each step sent a searing jolt of pain to my brain. I do not like pain one bit. My pace dropped off. I set each foot down as if on tacks.

"Only six miles to go," I had thought smugly as I breezed along. "Six miles is nothing. I can run six miles in my sleep." But the Marathon is not a place for smugness. Respect for that distance and for the human body that runs it is essential.

My respect returned as my pace dropped. The last two miles seemed interminable.

I began to feel like a failure. And this is where I learned the real meaning of fortitude: to keep on in the face of disappointment, to continue to do your best even when others are passing you. To see your hopes crushed and yet to continue. This is why I have as much respect for those who run and do not finish first as I have for the ones whose strength, endurance and training brings them first place.

At last I turned the corner and there was the Prudential Center and the finish line.

Newspaper reporters and TV cameras crowded into the street.

The crowd was wild.

I had finished 126th out of some four hundred fifty runners in a time of three hours, twenty-one minutes, and forty seconds.

Busloads of runners who had dropped out of the race passed waving, cheering, laughing.

I loved that crowd.

I loved my fellow runners.

I was supremely happy.

Governor Volpe himself appeared to shake my hand. I was honored.

The feeling that emerged from the crowd was that I was special not just because I had run the Marathon, but because I was a woman.

I don't think of myself as special, or rather, I think everyone is special in his or her unique way.

What I wanted was not the acclaim for myself, for I would rather have love, peace, good health, outlets for my creativity, and children.

What I want and wanted is a better world for all.

A better world begins with individual integrity.

As I turned to follow the other runners to the traditional post-marathon stew, the doors were shut.

I walked across the damp, cold parking garage alone.

That old lump came to my throat again. I knew there was more to be done to break down the subtle barriers of which I had so recently become aware, to restore harmony and end ignorance and fear.

Yet I had opened the door to a world of possibilities and had brought attention to running as a way of life.

The time was ripe. Once the idea was made public, other women began to filter in. More and more women every year until six years later, in 1972, even the officials recognized women as "official."

I was to run two more years, 1967 and 1968, my beloved Boston Marathon.

I sought the quiet places I'd left, the mountain trails, the vast blue sky, the nameless clouds, forests, deserts, and ocean beaches.

I returned to reestablish my bond with Nature, with the Source of all Being.

Once again running became a way to express joy.

I'm glad those who followed me have opened up competitive running to women. I am even more pleased that people, men and women, everywhere are finding running as a way of life.

Especially I appreciate the people who quietly and privately go about their lives and running without the thought or possibility of winning marathons, but whose balance, courage, and persever-ance is heroic, perhaps more so for being unnoticed and unacclaimed.

People, ordinary people, are extraordinary, whether given credit or not.

Is the mountain flower less beautiful because it blooms unnoticed? I think not.

I believe in people and in the infinite goodness of all creation.

Bobbi Gibb Art

Bobbi Gibb is an exciting contemporary artist who creates bronze sculptures of the human form in action and portrait busts; vividly colored murals; and subtle, impressionistic landscapes, which reflect her deep love of both humanity and nature.

Bobbi's artwork reflects the human and divine spirit and her point of view on the transcendent source of all being. From life-like busts and full body sculptures detailing the human form in an exacting manner to expansive murals that display an explosion of nature as she sees it in her imagination, Bobbi's work explores all facets of nature.

For more information, or to commission artwork, visit:

http://www.bobbigibbart.net/

Bobbi Gibb
Marathon Sculpture Project

Join Joan Samuelson, Bill Rodgers, Meb Keflezighi, and a dozen other Boston Marathon winners by making a donation to the Bobbi Gibb Marathon Sculpture Project.

Boston currently has several sculptures of male marathon runners, but none of women runners. Your contribution will help support the creation of a sculpture by the Boston Marathon's first woman runner (Bobbi Gibb, 1966) that will honor women's running and the proud tradition of women in the Boston Marathon.

To donate, visit FirstGiving.com and search for "Gibb sculpture" or send a check to:

Bobbi Gibb Marathon Sculpture Project
c/o 26.2 Foundation
P.O. Box 820
Hopkinton, MA 01748

Thanks for your help!

16631494R00039

Printed in Great Britain
by Amazon